MW00861343

INTROVERT

PETER PAUPER PRESS, INC.
WHITE PLAINS, NEW YORK

PETER PAUPER PRESS
Fine Books and Gifts Since 1928

Our Company

In 1928, at the age of twenty-two, Peter Beilenson began printing books on a small press in the basement of his parents' home in Larchmont, New York. Peter—and later, his wife, Edna—sought to create fine books that sold at "prices even a pauper could afford."

Today, still family owned and operated, Peter Pauper Press continues to honor our founders' legacy—and our customers' expectations—of beauty, quality, and value.

Cover illustration used under license from Shutterstock.com
Designed by Heather Zschock

202 Mamaroneck Avenue
White Plains, NY 10601 USA

ISBN 978-1-4413-2933-2
Printed in China
7 6 5 4 3 2 1

Visit us at www.peterpauper.com

IN ORDER TO UNDERSTAND THE WORLD,
ONE HAS TO TURN AWAY FROM IT ON OCCASION.

–Albert Camus

MY IMAGINATION FUNCTIONS MUCH BETTER WHEN I DON'T HAVE TO SPEAK TO PEOPLE.

–Patricia Highsmith

YOU HAVE A GRAND GIFT FOR SILENCE, WATSON.
IT MAKES YOU QUITE INVALUABLE AS A COMPANION.

–The Adventures of Sherlock Holmes, *Sir Arthur Conan Doyle*

I HAVE TO BE ALONE VERY OFTEN. I'D BE QUITE HAPPY IF I SPENT FROM SATURDAY NIGHT UNTIL MONDAY MORNING ALONE IN MY APARTMENT. THAT'S HOW I REFUEL.

–Audrey Hepburn

SOLITUDE GIVES BIRTH TO THE ORIGINAL IN US,
TO BEAUTY UNFAMILIAR AND PERILOUS—TO POETRY.

–Thomas Mann

I LOVE TO BE ALONE. I NEVER FOUND THE COMPANION THAT WAS SO COMPANIONABLE AS SOLITUDE.

–Henry David Thoreau

CHERISH YOUR SOLITUDE. TAKE TRAINS BY YOURSELF TO PLACES YOU HAVE NEVER BEEN.
SLEEP OUT ALONE UNDER THE STARS. LEARN HOW TO DRIVE A STICK SHIFT.
GO SO FAR AWAY THAT YOU STOP BEING AFRAID OF NOT COMING BACK.

–Eve Ensler

WRITING IS SOMETHING YOU DO ALONE. IT'S A PROFESSION FOR INTROVERTS WHO WANT TO TELL YOU A STORY BUT DON'T WANT TO MAKE EYE CONTACT WHILE DOING IT.

–John Green

SILENCE IS THE LANGUAGE OF GOD, ALL ELSE IS POOR TRANSLATION.

–Rumi

THE INWARD LIFE MIGHT BE AS MANIFOLD, AS VARIED, AS RICH WITH EXPERIENCE, AS THE LIFE OF ONE WHO CONQUERED REALMS AND EXPLORED UNKNOWN LANDS.

–*W. Somerset Maugham*

SPEAK ONLY IF IT IMPROVES UPON THE SILENCE.

–Mahatma Gandhi

PART OF DOING SOMETHING IS LISTENING. WE ARE LISTENING. TO THE SUN. TO THE STARS. TO THE WIND.

–Madeleine L'Engle

IF YOU ARE ALONE, YOU BELONG ENTIRELY TO YOURSELF.

–Leonardo da Vinci

IN A GENTLE WAY, YOU CAN SHAKE THE WORLD.

–Mahatma Gandhi

I LIVE IN THAT SOLITUDE WHICH IS PAINFUL IN YOUTH, BUT DELICIOUS IN THE YEARS OF MATURITY.

–Albert Einstein

TO BE LEFT ALONE IS THE MOST PRECIOUS THING ONE CAN ASK OF THE MODERN WORLD.

–Anthony Burgess

HOW MUCH BETTER TO SIT BY MYSELF LIKE THE SOLITARY SEABIRD THAT OPENS ITS WINGS ON THE STAKE. LET ME SIT HERE FOR EVER WITH BARE THINGS, THIS COFFEE CUP, THIS KNIFE, THIS FORK, THINGS IN THEMSELVES, MYSELF BEING MYSELF.

–Virginia Woolf

I'LL READ MY BOOKS AND I'LL DRINK COFFEE AND I'LL LISTEN TO MUSIC, AND I'LL BOLT THE DOOR.

–J.D. Salinger

I AM THE CAT WHO WALKS BY HIMSELF, AND ALL PLACES ARE ALIKE TO ME.

–Rudyard Kipling

SOLITUDE IS RICHNESS OF SELF.

–May Sarton

THE IMAGINATION NEEDS MOODLING—LONG, INEFFICIENT HAPPY IDLING, DAWDLING AND PUTTERING.

–Brenda Ueland

READING IS THAT FRUITFUL MIRACLE OF A COMMUNICATION IN THE MIDST OF SOLITUDE.

–Marcel Proust

A SENSIBLE MAN OUGHT TO FIND SUFFICIENT COMPANY IN HIMSELF.

–Emily Brontë

LOVE IS ESSENTIAL, GREGARIOUSNESS IS OPTIONAL.

–Susan Cain

THEN STIRS THE FEELING INFINITE, SO FELT IN SOLITUDE, WHERE WE ARE LEAST ALONE.

–Lord Byron

IT IS IN YOUR POWER TO WITHDRAW YOURSELF WHENEVER YOU DESIRE. PERFECT TRANQUILITY WITHIN CONSISTS IN THE GOOD ORDERING OF THE MIND, THE REALM OF YOUR OWN.

–Marcus Aurelius

THE SOUL THAT SEES BEAUTY MAY SOMETIMES WALK ALONE.

–Johann Wolfgang von Goethe

BUT THERE IS GREATER COMFORT IN THE SUBSTANCE OF SILENCE THAN IN THE ANSWER TO A QUESTION.

–*Thomas Merton*

SOLITUDE PRODUCES ORIGINALITY, BOLD AND ASTONISHING BEAUTY, POETRY.

–Thomas Mann

TO LIE SOMETIMES ON THE GRASS UNDER THE TREES ON A SUMMER'S DAY, LISTENING TO THE MURMUR OF WATER, OR WATCHING THE CLOUDS FLOAT ACROSS THE SKY, IS BY NO MEANS A WASTE OF TIME.

–John Lubbock

FOR THOSE WHO KNOW THE VALUE OF AND EXQUISITE TASTE OF SOLITARY FREEDOM (FOR ONE IS ONLY FREE WHEN ALONE), THE ACT OF LEAVING IS THE BRAVEST AND MOST BEAUTIFUL OF ALL.

–Isabelle Eberhardt

HOW CAN YOU HEAR YOUR SOUL IF EVERYONE IS TALKING?

–Mary Doria Russell

KNOWING HOW TO BE SOLITARY IS CENTRAL TO THE ART OF LOVING. WHEN WE CAN BE ALONE, WE CAN BE WITH OTHERS WITHOUT USING THEM AS A MEANS OF ESCAPE.

–bell hooks

I LOVE SILENCE. I SEEK AND CREATE IT AT EVERY OPPORTUNITY. I NEED IT TO WORK.

–Anne Lamott

THE SECRET OF A GOOD OLD AGE IS SIMPLY AN HONORABLE PACT WITH SOLITUDE.

–Gabriel García Márquez

KEEP INVIOLATE AN AREA OF LIGHT AND PEACE WITHIN YOU.

–Corazon Aquino

THIS WAS MY MOMENT TO LOOK FOR THE KIND OF HEALING AND PEACE THAT CAN ONLY COME FROM SOLITUDE.

–Elizabeth Gilbert

I NEED THE SUNSHINE AND THE PAVING STONES OF THE STREETS WITHOUT COMPANIONS, WITHOUT CONVERSATION, FACE TO FACE WITH MYSELF, WITH ONLY THE MUSIC OF MY HEART FOR COMPANY.

–Henry Miller

HOW GRACIOUS, HOW BENIGN, IS SOLITUDE.

–William Wordsworth

SILENCE IS A SOURCE OF GREAT STRENGTH.

–Lao Tzu